USING MATHS

FLY A JUMBO JET

by Wendy Clemson, David Clemson
and Chris Perry

KU-556-971

USING
MATHS
FLY A JUMBO JET

Copyright © ticktock Entertainment Ltd 2004

First published in Great Britain in 2004 by ticktock Media Ltd.,
Unit 2, Orchard Business Centre, North Farm Road, Tunbridge Wells, Kent, TN2 3XF

ISBN 1 86007 545 2 pbk
ISBN 1 86007 551 7 hbk
Printed in China

A CIP catalogue record for this book is available from the British Library.
All rights reserved. No part of this publication may be reproduced, copied, stored in a retrieval system
or transmitted in any form or by any means electronic, mechanical, photocopying, recording or otherwise
without prior written permission of the copyright owner.

With thanks to our consultants: Jenni Back and Liz Pumfrey from the NRICH Project,
Cambridge University and Debra Voege.
With special thanks to Lorna Cowan.

WENDY CLEMSON

Wendy is experienced in working with and for children, and has been writing full-time since 1989. Her publications, which now exceed one hundred, have been written for children and sometimes their parents and teachers. In her many maths books, the aim is always to present the reader with challenges that are fun to do.

DAVID CLEMSON

David has wide-ranging experience as a writer and educationalist. His publications list is prodigious. In collaboration with Wendy, David has worked on many maths books for children. He is fascinated by maths and logic puzzles and is keen for the reader to enjoy them too.

CHRIS PERRY

Chris is a qualified pilot and instructor. He works at the Oxford Aviation Training College, teaching prospective pilots to fly a wide range of aircraft, including commercial airliners, such as the Boeing 747-400 – the jumbo jet.

CONTENTS

NUMERACY WORK COVERED IN THIS BOOK:

CALCULATIONS:
Throughout this book there are opportunities to practise **addition, subtraction, multiplication** and **division** using both mental calculation strategies and pencil and paper methods.

NUMBERS AND THE NUMBER SYSTEM:
- COMPARING & ORDERING NUMBERS: pgs. 6, 18
- FRACTIONS: pgs. 10, 14
- READING NUMBERS IN WORDS AND FIGURES: pg. 6

SOLVING 'REAL LIFE' PROBLEMS:
- CHOOSING THE OPERATION: pgs. 8, 10, 12, 14, 16, 18, 21, 22
- MEASURES: pgs. 11, 12, 14, 16, 18, 22, 25
- TIME: pgs. 12, 17, 21, 22

HANDLING DATA:
- BAR CHARTS: pg. 8
- BAR LINE CHARTS: pg. 24
- USING TABLES/CHARTS/DIAGRAMS: pgs. 6, 8, 10, 11, 12, 18

MEASURES:
- RELATIONSHIPS BETWEEN UNITS OF MEASUREMENT: pg. 25
- USING METRIC/IMPERIAL MEASUREMENTS: pgs. 6, 10, 11, 12, 14, 16, 17, 18, 21, 22, 23, 25
- VOCABULARY (time): pgs. 14, 16, 17, 22, 23, 24

SHAPE AND SPACE:
- 2-D SHAPES: pg. 27
- 3-D SHAPES: pg. 15
- COMPASS DIRECTIONS: pg. 12
- GRID CO-ORDINATES: pg. 26

HOW TO USE THIS BOOK

Maths is important in the lives of people everywhere. We use maths when we play a game, ride a bike, go shopping – in fact, all the time! Everyone needs to use maths at work. You may not realise it, but a pilot would use maths to fly a jumbo jet! With this book you will get the chance to try lots of exciting maths activities using real life data and facts about planes and the work of airline pilots. Practise your maths and numeracy skills and experience the thrill of what it's really like to fly a jumbo jet.

This exciting maths book is very easy to use – check out what's inside!

Fun to read information about airliners and the work of airline pilots.

MATHS ACTIVITIES

Look for the
PILOT ASSESSMENT.
You will find real life maths activities and questions to try.

To answer some of the questions, you will need to collect data from a DATA BOX. Sometimes, you will need to collect facts and data from the text or from charts and diagrams.

Be prepared! You will need a pen or pencil and a notebook for your workings and answers.

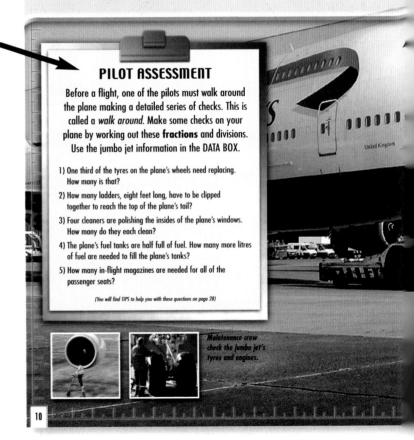

THE AMAZING JUMBO JET

You have reached the rank of First Officer, and you are now an experienced pilot. Today, you will be flying the fastest **commercial airliner** in service – the Boeing 747-400, or jumbo jet. This amazing plane flies at MACH .85 – this means it flies at 85% of the speed of sound. A jumbo jet's tail is about the same height as a six storey building, and its wings are so large, 45 family cars could park on them! Pilots have to arrive at the airport at least 80 minutes before a flight to carry out their pre-flight preparations. Start your preparations by taking your PILOT ASSESSMENT.

PILOT ASSESSMENT

Before a flight, one of the pilots must walk around the plane making a detailed series of checks. This is called a *walk around*. Make some checks on your plane by working out these **fractions** and divisions. Use the jumbo jet information in the DATA BOX.

1) One third of the tyres on the plane's wheels need replacing. How many is that?
2) How many ladders, eight feet long, have to be clipped together to reach the top of the plane's tail?
3) Four cleaners are polishing the insides of the plane's windows. How many do they each clean?
4) The plane's fuel tanks are half full of fuel. How many more litres of fuel are needed to fill the plane's tanks?
5) How many in-flight magazines are needed for all of the passenger seats?

(You will find TIPS to help you with these questions on page 28)

Maintenance crew check the jumbo jet's tyres and engines.

10

DATA BOX

If you see one of these boxes, there will be important data inside that will help you with the maths activities.

MATHS ACTIVITIES

Feeling confident? Try these extra **CHALLENGE QUESTIONS.**

IF YOU NEED HELP...

TIPS FOR MATHS SUCCESS

On pages 28 – 29 you will find lots of tips to help you with your maths work.

ANSWERS

Turn to pages 30 – 31 to check your answers.
(Try all the activities and questions before you take a look at the answers.)

GLOSSARY

On page 32 there is a glossary of aviation words and a glossary of maths words. The glossary words appear **in bold** in the text.

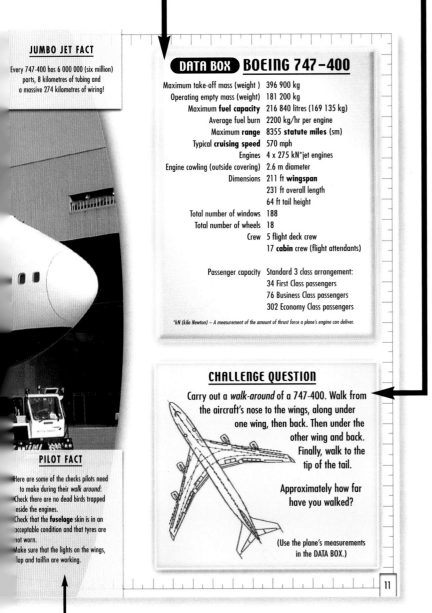

JUMBO JET FACT

Every 747-400 has 6 000 000 (six million) parts, 8 kilometres of tubing and a massive 274 kilometres of wiring!

DATA BOX BOEING 747–400

Maximum take-off mass (weight)	396 900 kg
Operating empty mass (weight)	181 200 kg
Maximum **fuel capacity**	216 840 litres (169 135 kg)
Average fuel burn	2200 kg/hr per engine
Maximum **range**	8355 **statute miles** (sm)
Typical **cruising speed**	570 mph
Engines	4 x 275 kN*jet engines
Engine cowling (outside covering)	2.6 m diameter
Dimensions	211 ft **wingspan**
	231 ft overall length
	64 ft tail height
Total number of windows	188
Total number of wheels	18
Crew	5 flight deck crew
	17 **cabin** crew (flight attendants)
Passenger capacity	Standard 3 class arrangement:
	34 First Class passengers
	76 Business Class passengers
	302 Economy Class passengers

*kN (kilo Newton) – A measurement of the amount of thrust force a plane's engine can deliver.

CHALLENGE QUESTION

Carry out a *walk-around* of a 747-400. Walk from the aircraft's nose to the wings, along under one wing, then back. Then under the other wing and back. Finally, walk to the tip of the tail.

Approximately how far have you walked?

(Use the plane's measurements in the DATA BOX.)

PILOT FACT

Here are some of the checks pilots need to make during their *walk around*:
Check there are no dead birds trapped inside the engines.
Check that the **fuselage** skin is in an acceptable condition and that tyres are not worn.
Make sure that the lights on the wings, flap and tailfin are working.

Fun to read facts about planes and flying.

11

LEARNING TO FLY AN AIRLINER

Trainee pilots are called cadets, they learn to fly using **flight simulators**. Cadets have to sit examinations and spend 200 hours flying real planes before they can graduate. To become a pilot you need to study **aerodynamics**, **navigation**, radio communication and even **meteorology**. All the training is worth it though, because there are some amazing planes out there just waiting to take off! During their careers, pilots learn to fly lots of different aircraft. Today, you are in the flight simulator. Look at the question on the clipboard and take your CADET PILOT ASSESSMENT.

CADET PILOT ASSESSMENT

In the DATA BOX you will see information about four **commercial airliners**. Can you work out which of the four aircraft has been programmed into the flight simulator for your training flight?

(You need to compare the aircraft.)

- It has a **wingspan** that is less than the wingspan of the Boeing 777.
- It has a **range** greater than the Airbus A320.
- It is third largest in order of tail height.
- It is smallest in order of take-off mass (weight).
- It has engines that are approximately 100 kN.

Which aircraft is programmed into the flight simulator?

(You will find information about UNITS OF MEASUREMENT on page 29)

CHALLENGE QUESTION

Which of these is the maximum **fuel capacity** of the Airbus A320?
a) Twenty three thousand six hundred and eighty litres
b) Twenty three thousand eight hundred and sixty litres
c) Two thousand three hundred and eighty six litres

(You will find a TIP to help you with this question on page 28)

FLIGHT TRAINING FACT

Flight simulators are machines that use computer programmes to create flying conditions just like the real thing. Pilots use flight simulators to practise taking off and landing, and to practise dealing with **turbulence**, thunderstorms and emergencies, such as an engine failure!

DATA BOX AIRCRAFT SPECIFICATIONS

Airbus A320

Max take-off mass (weight)	73 500 kg
Maximum fuel capacity	23 860 litres
Maximum range	3050 **statute miles** (sm)
Typical **cruising speed**	530 mph
Engines	2 x 106 kN*jet engines
Dimensions	112 ft wingspan
	123 ft overall length
	38 ft tail height

Airbus A340

Max take-off mass (weight)	275 000 kg
Maximum fuel capacity	155 040 litres
Maximum range	9200 statute miles (sm)
Typical cruising speed	555 mph
Engines	4 x 145 kN*jet engines
Dimensions	197 ft wingspan
	195 ft overall length
	54 ft tail height

Boeing 737

Max take-off mass (weight)	65 090 kg
Maximum fuel capacity	26 035 litres
Maximum range	3510 statute miles (sm)
Typical cruising speed	530 mph
Engines	2 x 101 kN*jet engines
Dimensions	112 ft wingspan
	102 ft overall length
	41 ft tail height

Boeing 777

Max take-off mass (weight)	299 370 kg
Maximum fuel capacity	171 160 litres
Maximum range	6850 statute miles (sm)
Typical cruising speed	560 mph
Engines	2 x 421 kN*jet engines
Dimensions	200 ft wingspan
	242 ft overall length
	60 ft tail height

*kN (kilo Newton) – A measurement of the amount of thrust force a plane's engine can deliver.

TRAVELLING THE WORLD

Airline pilots are able to fly into any airport in the world. They use special charts, called Jeppesen Charts, that show them the length and width of the runways and details about the height and location of any mountains or tall buildings in the area. Today, you are the Second Officer (the junior pilot) on a flight to Atlanta, USA. Your plane is about to land at Hartsfield International Airport – the busiest airport in the world! Over 44 800 people work at Hartsfield, and flights take off and land 24 hours a day. It is now time to take your SECOND OFFICER ASSESSMENT.

SECOND OFFICER ASSESSMENT

In the DATA BOX you will see the enormous numbers of passengers that go through the world's busiest airports every year. The passenger numbers for six of the airports have been put into a **bar chart**, but the airport name labels are missing.

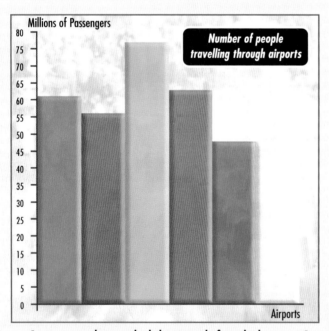

Can you work out which bar stands for which airport?

(To get you started, the red bar stands for the number of passengers going through the Los Angeles International Airport.)

(You will find TIPS to help you with this activity on page 28)

CHALLENGE QUESTION

If you wanted to know how many passengers went through each of the airports in a week, what would you need to do?

(You will find a TIP to help you with this question on page 28)

AIRPORT FACT

Hartsfield International Airport produces over 57 **tonnes** of rubbish every day!

AIRPORT FACT

Items handed in to the Heathrow Airport lost property office include a laptop computer worth £4000, a briefcase containing £37 000 in cash, a suitcase of dead fish and a false leg!

DATA BOX WORLD'S TOP 10 BUSIEST AIRPORTS

Number of passengers per year:

1st Hartsfield International, Atlanta, USA	77 000 000
2nd O'Hare International, Chicago, USA	67 000 000
3rd Heathrow Airport, London, UK	63 000 000
4th Haneda International, Tokyo, Japan	61 000 000
5th Los Angeles International, Los Angeles, USA	56 000 000
6th Dallas Fort Worth International, Dallas, USA	53 000 000
7th Frankfurt Airport, Frankfurt, Germany	48 000 000
8th Charles de Gaulle International, Paris, France	48 000 000
9th Schiphol International, Amsterdam, Netherlands	41 000 000
10th Denver International, Denver, USA	36 000 000

Hartsfield International Airport viewed from a plane.

AIRPORT FACT

Over 26 000 cups of tea, 6500 pints of beer and 6500 sandwiches are purchased by visitors and passengers at Heathrow Airport every day!

Concorde lands at Heathrow Airport for the last time in October 2003.

THE AMAZING JUMBO JET

You have reached the rank of First Officer, and you are now an experienced pilot. Today, you will be flying the fastest **commercial airliner** in service – the Boeing 747-400, or jumbo jet. This amazing plane flies at MACH .85 – this means it flies at 85% of the speed of sound. A jumbo jet's tail is about the same height as a six storey building, and its wings are so large, 45 family cars could park on them! Pilots have to arrive at the airport at least 80 minutes before a flight to carry out their pre-flight preparations. Start your preparations by taking your PILOT ASSESSMENT.

PILOT ASSESSMENT

Before a flight, one of the pilots must walk around the plane making a detailed series of checks. This is called a *walk around*. Make some checks on your plane by working out these **fractions** and divisions. Use the jumbo jet information in the DATA BOX.

1) One third of the tyres on the plane's wheels need replacing. How many is that?

2) How many ladders, eight feet long, have to be clipped together to reach the top of the plane's tail?

3) Four cleaners are polishing the insides of the plane's windows. How many do they each clean?

4) The plane's fuel tanks are half full of fuel. How many more litres of fuel are needed to fill the plane's tanks?

5) How many in-flight magazines are needed for all of the passenger seats?

(You will find TIPS to help you with these questions on page 28)

Maintenance crew check the jumbo jet's tyres and engines.

JUMBO JET FACT

Every 747-400 has 6 000 000 (six million) parts, 8 kilometres of tubing and a massive 274 kilometres of wiring!

DATA BOX BOEING 747-400

Maximum take-off mass (weight)	396 900 kg
Operating empty mass (weight)	181 200 kg
Maximum **fuel capacity**	216 840 litres (169 135 kg)
Average fuel burn	2200 kg/hr per engine
Maximum **range**	8355 **statute miles** (sm)
Typical **cruising speed**	570 mph
Engines	4 x 275 kN*jet engines
Engine cowling (outside covering)	2.6 m diameter
Dimensions	211 ft **wingspan**
	231 ft overall length
	64 ft tail height
Total number of windows	188
Total number of wheels	18
Crew	5 flight deck crew
	17 **cabin** crew (flight attendants)
Passenger capacity	Standard 3 class arrangement:
	34 First Class passengers
	76 Business Class passengers
	302 Economy Class passengers

*kN (kilo Newton) – A measurement of the amount of thrust force a plane's engine can deliver.

PILOT FACT

Here are some of the checks pilots need to make during their *walk around*:
• Check there are no dead birds trapped inside the engines.
• Check that the **fuselage** skin is in an acceptable condition and that tyres are not worn.
• Make sure that the lights on the wings, flap and tailfin are working.

CHALLENGE QUESTION

Carry out a *walk-around* of a 747-400. Walk from the aircraft's nose to the wings, along under one wing, then back. Then under the other wing and back. Finally, walk to the tip of the tail.

Approximately how far have you walked?

(Use the plane's measurements in the DATA BOX.)

MAKING A FLIGHT PLAN

One of the most important pre-flight jobs that a pilot does is prepare a **flight plan.** Today, your airline wants you to fly from Heathrow Airport in London, to John F. Kennedy Airport (JFK) in New York City. The flight plan will show important information about the flight, such as how much fuel will be used, the speed that the plane will travel at, the direction of the wind and how long the flight will take. The information in the flight plan will be input into the plane's computer system. You will need to use times and distances to complete your next PILOT ASSESSMENT.

PILOT ASSESSMENT

The map and DATA BOX on these pages show the types of information that pilots use to help them plan their flights. Using the journey times and distances in the DATA BOX, work out the answers to these questions:

1) How much further is it in miles from Paris to Cairo than from Moscow to Rome?

2) What is the difference in journey time between New York to Los Angeles and Los Angeles to Atlanta?

3) You are planning to fly from London to Cairo via Paris. What is the distance that you will travel?

You are flying from London to Atlanta, via New York and Los Angeles.

4) How far will you travel?

5) What is the total journey time?

(You will find a TIP to help you with questions 2 and 5 on page 28)

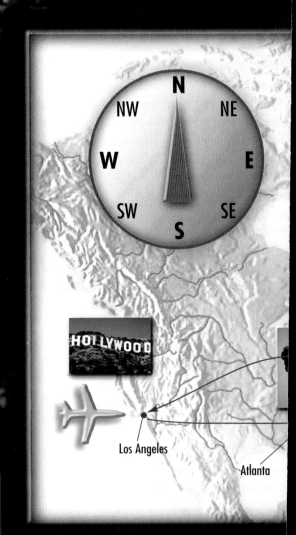

CHALLENGE QUESTIONS
Use the compass on the map to answer the following questions:

a) Which city on the map is SW of Washington?
b) Which city on the map is NE of Rome?
c) Which cities on the map are south-east of Paris?

FLIGHT FACT

Pilots are trained to fly around the world using *air corridors* – imaginary roads in the sky.

JUMBO JET FACT

Between them, all the 747s in service have flown 35 billion miles. That's enough miles to make 74 000 trips to the Moon and back!

DATA BOX FLIGHT TIMES AND DISTANCES

Journey	Distance (miles)	Journey time
London to New York	3444	6 hours
New York to Boston	186	30 minutes
New York to Washington	228	45 minutes
New York to Los Angeles	2471	4 hours 30 minutes
Los Angeles to Atlanta	1944	3 hours 40 minutes
London to Paris	216	23 minutes
Paris to Cairo	2363	4 hours 15 minutes
Moscow to Rome	1893	3 hours 30 minutes

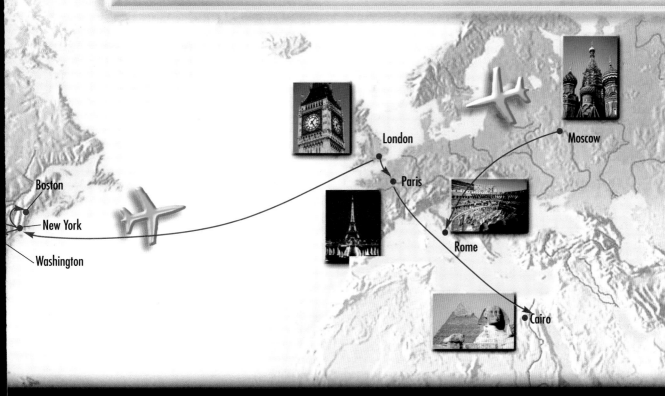

Boston
New York
Washington
London
Paris
Moscow
Rome
Cairo

IMPORTANT PRE-FLIGHT CALCULATIONS

During their pre-flight preparations, pilots must calculate how much fuel they will need for the journey. A jumbo jet has an incredible **cruising speed** of 570 mph. At this speed, the plane's four engines will burn approximately 9000 kg of fuel every hour. A normal car would have to drive at top speed, non-stop day and night, for over a month, to use as much fuel as a jumbo jet uses in one hour! All aircraft must carry enough fuel to reach their destination and then some spare fuel in case there is an emergency, and the flight is diverted to another airport. Before you fly, you will need to check how much fuel is needed for your journey.

PILOT ASSESSMENT

- *You will be flying a jumbo jet which burns 9000 kg of fuel per hour.*
- *It will take 6 hours to get from Heathrow Airport, London to JFK Airport, New York.*

1) What weight of fuel is needed?

- *If there is an emergency at JFK, you may be diverted to an airport in Boston or Washington.*

2) If you divert to Boston airport, you will need fuel for a further half hour. What weight of fuel is that?

3) If you divert to Washington, you will need fuel for an extra three quarters of an hour. What weight of fuel is that?

A tanker delivers fuel to a jumbo jet.

*A view of the **cockpit** in a jumbo jet.*

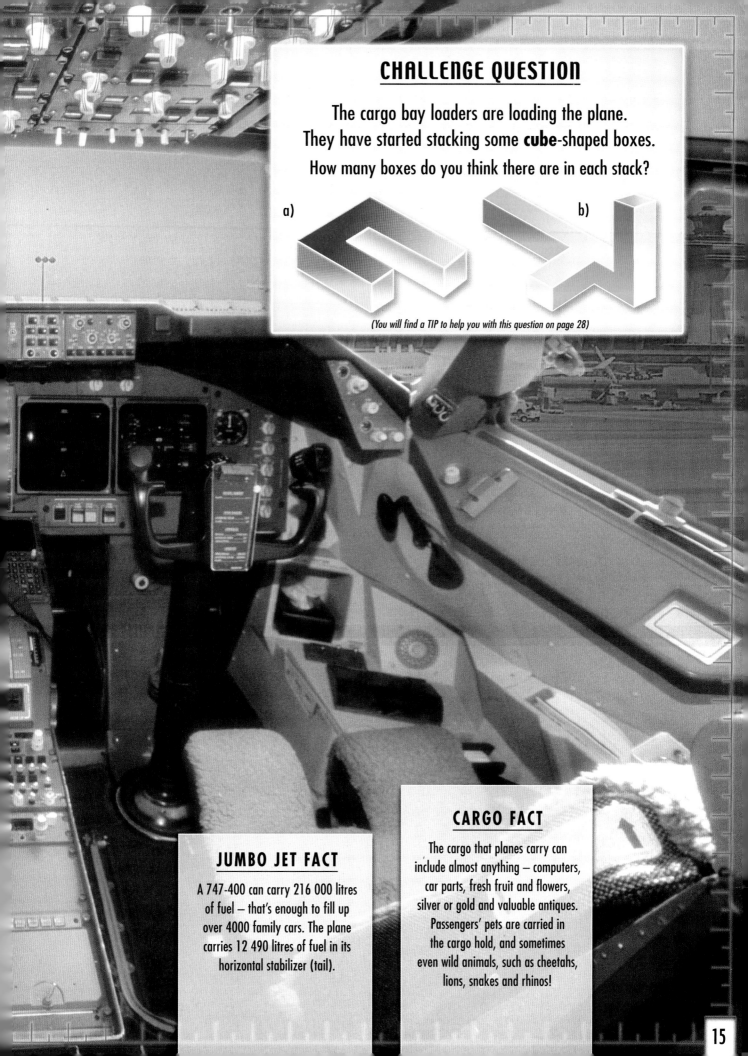

CHALLENGE QUESTION

The cargo bay loaders are loading the plane.
They have started stacking some **cube**-shaped boxes.
How many boxes do you think there are in each stack?

a)

b)

(You will find a TIP to help you with this question on page 28)

JUMBO JET FACT

A 747-400 can carry 216 000 litres
of fuel – that's enough to fill up
over 4000 family cars. The plane
carries 12 490 litres of fuel in its
horizontal stabilizer (tail).

CARGO FACT

The cargo that planes carry can
include almost anything – computers,
car parts, fresh fruit and flowers,
silver or gold and valuable antiques.
Passengers' pets are carried in
the cargo hold, and sometimes
even wild animals, such as cheetahs,
lions, snakes and rhinos!

COUNTDOWN TO TAKE-OFF

Working as a team with the captain, you have filed your **flight plan**, calculated your fuel, examined the weather forecasts and checked your aircraft — both the outside of the plane and the **flight instruments** in the **cockpit**. You are now sitting in the right-hand seat in the cockpit. Both pilot seats have the same controls, but today, the captain is PNF (Pilot Non Flying). This means you are the PF (Pilot Flying) — you will be flying the plane! There is one more PILOT ASSESSMENT to work through before take-off.

PILOT ASSESSMENT

The most your aircraft and its contents can weigh at take-off is 397 000 kg. You must not overload your plane!

- *The empty plane weighs 181 200 kg.*
- *You have filled up with 67 000 kg of fuel.*

1) What is the weight of the empty plane and its fuel?

2) What is the maximum that the cargo, passengers and crew can now weigh?

- *When your plane takes off, it will climb 3000 ft every minute.*

3) How high will you be after 5 minutes?

4) How high will you be after 10 minutes?

5) After 12 minutes, the plane levels out. What is the plane's altitude (height above ground level)?

A 747-400 taxis onto the runway.

Airliners wait in a queue to be cleared for take-off.

Leaving the ground.

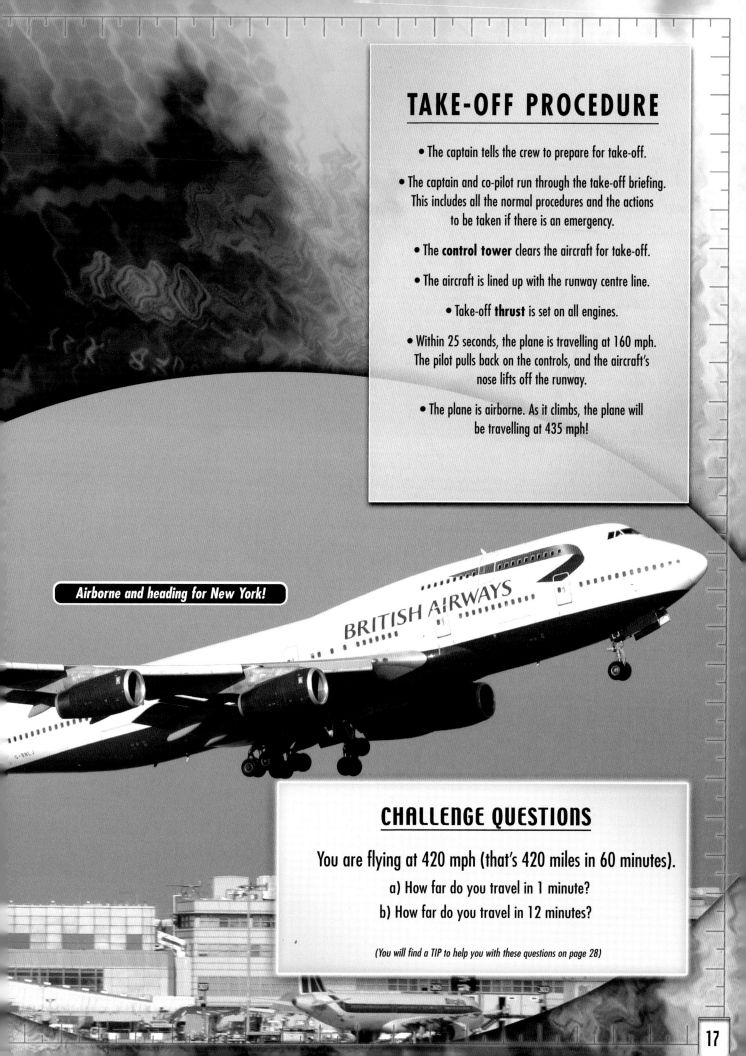

TAKE-OFF PROCEDURE

- The captain tells the crew to prepare for take-off.

- The captain and co-pilot run through the take-off briefing. This includes all the normal procedures and the actions to be taken if there is an emergency.

- The **control tower** clears the aircraft for take-off.

- The aircraft is lined up with the runway centre line.

- Take-off **thrust** is set on all engines.

- Within 25 seconds, the plane is travelling at 160 mph. The pilot pulls back on the controls, and the aircraft's nose lifts off the runway.

- The plane is airborne. As it climbs, the plane will be travelling at 435 mph!

Airborne and heading for New York!

CHALLENGE QUESTIONS

You are flying at 420 mph (that's 420 miles in 60 minutes).

a) How far do you travel in 1 minute?

b) How far do you travel in 12 minutes?

(You will find a TIP to help you with these questions on page 28)

TIME FOR A BREAK

Your aircraft is now at **cruising speed** and the journey is under way. In the **cabin**, the passengers are watching TV and waiting to have their dinner. Some of the flight attendants are busy in the galley (the plane's kitchen). They are heating up and preparing the meals that were loaded on board the plane. Other flight attendants are serving the food and fetching drinks for all the passengers. During a flight, the attendants will also bring the flight crew drinks and food. The pilots will take it in turn to stop work and have something to eat. It's time to have a break and try another PILOT ASSESSMENT.

PILOT ASSESSMENT

Jumbo jets carry a lot of food and drink.
In the DATA BOX you will see a list of items
that are carried on a 747 flight.
Use this information to answer these questions:

1) In total, how many bottles of cola are there on board?

2) Ten bottles of bitter lemon are drunk during a flight. What **volume** of bitter lemon is that?

3) In total, how many cartons of fruit juice are there on board?

4) ¼ of all the apple juice is drunk during a flight. How many litres is that?

5) How many more bottles of sparkling water than soda water are on board?

Check your knowledge of the signs for *less than* and *more than*. Is each of these statements true or false?

6) Number of cartons of orange juice > number of cartons of tomato juice.

7) Number of diet tonic waters < number of ginger ales.

8) Number of tonic waters (regular and diet) > number of diet colas.

(You will find a TIP to help you with questions 6, 7 and 8 on page 28)

A flight attendant serves the passengers drinks and food.

CHALLENGE QUESTIONS

48 passengers want a cup of tea.

a) How many pots of tea need to be made?

b) How much water will be used?

FLIGHT ATTENDANTS FACT

Flight attendants don't just serve food and drinks to the passengers. They make sure that all the plane's safety rules are followed and will help passengers if there is an emergency situation.

IN-FLIGHT FACT

There are 48 000 food and non-food items packed on every jumbo jet flight! This includes bottles of wine and champagne, fresh fruit, cakes, cheese, sandwiches and hot meals, such as soup, roast beef and pasta. The non-food items include newspapers, duvets, sleeper suits, games for children and, of course, sick bags!

The cabin of a 747-400

DATA BOX — IN THE GALLEY

SOFT DRINKS (all 0.15 litre bottles)

Cola	212	bottles
Diet cola	159	bottles
Bitter lemon	24	bottles
Soda water	22	bottles
Tonic water	143	bottles
Diet tonic water	10	bottles
Sparkling water	50	bottles
Ginger ale	94	bottles
Lemonade drinks	124	bottles

FRUIT JUICES (all 1 litre cartons)

Orange juice	59	cartons
Apple juice	20	cartons
Tomato juice	20	cartons

HOT DRINKS

- 240 large tea bags
- 155 packets of coffee
- Each packet of coffee and each large tea bag makes a 1.5 litre pot of coffee or tea.
- Each 1.5 litre pot gives 12 cups of tea or coffee.

IN-FLIGHT FACT

Many jumbo jets now have seat back televisions. Passengers can choose between 11 movie channels and 7 TV channels. First Class passengers can choose from a selection of videos, too.

BAD WEATHER AHEAD

During a flight, pilots need to carry out a number of routine checks. Sometimes your checks will show there has been a change in the wind speed. This could affect your **cruising speed**, making it slower or faster. If the wind speed increases, and there is a following wind (the wind is behind you), the plane will travel faster and use less fuel. If your cruising speed drops, it will take you longer to reach your destination. Sometimes you might pick up a really bad storm on the weather **radar**. It is best to divert around storms, but this uses more fuel. During a flight, you will have to be ready to deal with unexpected situations and be able to make quick in-flight calculations.

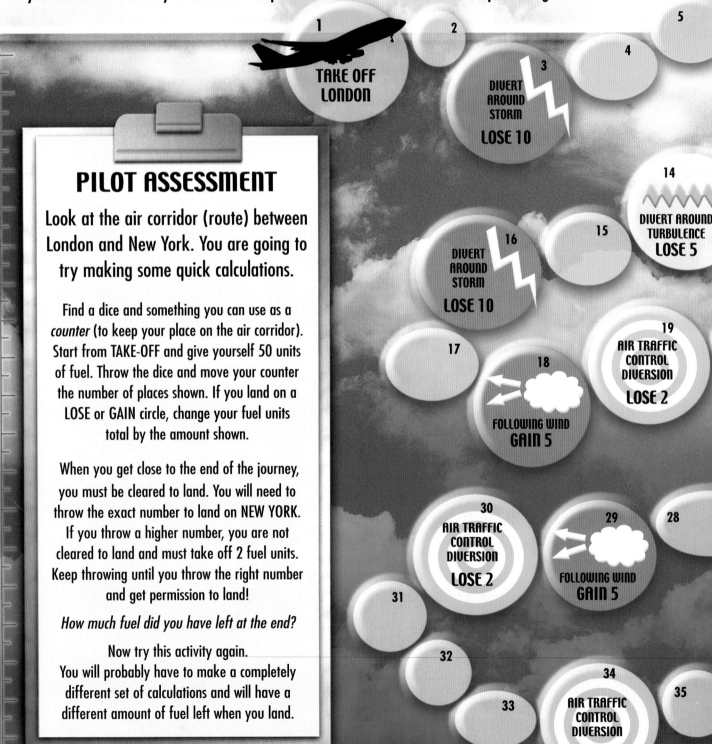

PILOT ASSESSMENT

Look at the air corridor (route) between London and New York. You are going to try making some quick calculations.

Find a dice and something you can use as a *counter* (to keep your place on the air corridor). Start from TAKE-OFF and give yourself 50 units of fuel. Throw the dice and move your counter the number of places shown. If you land on a LOSE or GAIN circle, change your fuel units total by the amount shown.

When you get close to the end of the journey, you must be cleared to land. You will need to throw the exact number to land on NEW YORK. If you throw a higher number, you are not cleared to land and must take off 2 fuel units. Keep throwing until you throw the right number and get permission to land!

How much fuel did you have left at the end?

Now try this activity again. You will probably have to make a completely different set of calculations and will have a different amount of fuel left when you land.

1 TAKE OFF LONDON
2
3 DIVERT AROUND STORM LOSE 10
4
5
14 DIVERT AROUND TURBULENCE LOSE 5
15
16 DIVERT AROUND STORM LOSE 10
17
18 FOLLOWING WIND GAIN 5
19 AIR TRAFFIC CONTROL DIVERSION LOSE 2
28
29 FOLLOWING WIND GAIN 5
30 AIR TRAFFIC CONTROL DIVERSION LOSE 2
31
32
33
34 AIR TRAFFIC CONTROL DIVERSION LOSE 2
35

FLIGHT FACT

Weather can make a big difference to the length of a flight. Before take-off, pilots check the weather forecasts for wind, thunderstorms and **turbulence** in all the areas they will be flying through.

AIR TRAFFIC CONTROL FACT

While they are flying, pilots are in contact with **air traffic controllers** at all times. ATCs make sure that planes stay a safe distance apart in the sky; they keep pilots informed about weather or other problems and they organise the flow of planes in and out of airports.

7
DIVERT AROUND STORM
LOSE 10

6

8
AIR TRAFFIC CONTROL DIVERSION
LOSE 2

9

13

12

11

10
DIVERT AROUND TURBULENCE
LOSE 5

21
AIR TRAFFIC CONTROL DIVERSION
LOSE 2

22

23

24
FOLLOWING WIND
GAIN 5

26
DIVERT AROUND STORM
LOSE 10

25

27

36
NEW YORK

When you throw a dice you can't control what happens. This is a bit like bad weather – pilots have no control over the weather, but they have to be able to make calculations to deal with it.

CHALLENGE QUESTIONS

It is 9:00 pm and you have one thousand miles still to fly to get to New York.

You are travelling at 500 mph.

a) How much longer will your journey take?

b) What time should you land in New York?

You check the radar and see a storm ahead. You decide to fly around the storm, but this diversion will add two hundred and fifty miles to your journey.

c) How much longer will the flight take?

d) What time will you land now?

Sometimes an aircraft cannot land where it originally planned. When this happens, the pilot has to make a quick decision about what to do. The time is 10:55 pm (22:55) and you are approaching New York. Suddenly you receive a call from the **air traffic controllers**. There has been a terrible storm in the area and an emergency has been declared. JFK Airport will be closed until 1:00 am (01:00). You now have to decide whether to circle, and wait for JFK to reopen, or divert to a different airport. It is time to do some quick thinking!

PILOT ASSESSMENT

Use the information on this clipboard to work out what to do.

- *Your aircraft uses 9000 kg of fuel every hour.*
- *Your in-flight computer shows you have 13 500 kg of fuel left.*
- *The clocks (below) show the current time.*

Do you wish to:

OPTION 1: Circle until JFK reopens at 1:00 am (01:00) and land here.
OPTION 2: Fly to Boston Airport which closes at 11:15 pm (23:15). It will take half an hour to fly to Boston Airport.
OPTION 3: Fly to Washington Airport which closes at 11:45 pm (23:45). It will take 45 minutes to fly to Washington Airport.

Which option did you choose?

(You will find a TIP to help you with this activity on page 29 and information about 24 HOUR CLOCKS.)

ANALOGUE CLOCK

DIGITAL CLOCK

22:55

JUMBO JET FACT

There are 365 lights, gauges and switches on the flight deck of the latest 747-400s.

747 FACTS

Some 747s have been used for special assignments:
- A specially modified 747 was used to carry the space shuttle between California and Florida.
- Two 747-200s have been used as Air Force One airplanes — the US president's special plane.
- There have been demonstrations of 747s being used as flying fuel tankers. They can refuel other planes in flight!

Ice and snow at JFK Airport.

Air traffic controllers notify pilots of the weather problems at the airport.

CHALLENGE QUESTION

If your plane had to circle (fly over) New York for two and a half hours, how much fuel would you need to do this?

YOU ARE CLEARED TO LAND

The flight is nearly over and you have successfully negotiated storms, **turbulence** and even an emergency diversion. You are now approaching the airport and the captain has just told the crew to prepare for landing. You have never landed at this airport before, but you are familiar with the runway and the area around the airport. This is because, like all pilots, you have practised landing at this airport in a **flight simulator**. The **control tower** has cleared you to land. You have just enough time to take a PILOT ASSESSMENT.

PILOT ASSESSMENT

From cruising at 24 500 feet, you wish to land in seven minutes. Here is a **bar line chart** showing your descent. You can see that after one minute the plane has descended 3500 feet and is at 21 000 feet.

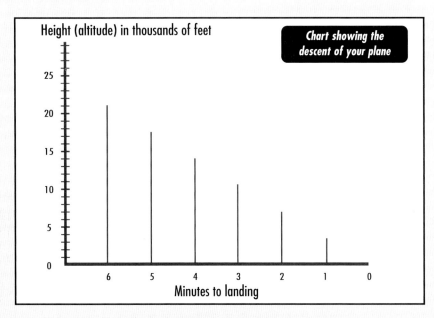

Height (altitude) in thousands of feet

Chart showing the descent of your plane

Minutes to landing

Now use the chart to answer the questions below:

1) How high is the plane after descending for 2 minutes?
2) After how many minutes of descent has the plane reached 10 500 feet?
3) What is the height of the plane at 2 minutes before landing?
4) When the plane has reached 14 000 feet, it is how many minutes from landing?
5) What is the height of the plane at three and a half minutes to landing?

(You will find a TIP to help you with these questions on page 29)

LANDING PROCEDURE

- The captain tells the crew to prepare for landing.

- The captain and co-pilot run through the landing briefing. This includes all the normal procedures and the actions to be taken if there is an emergency.

- The wing flaps and undercarriage (wheels) are lowered.

- The control tower at the airport clears the aircraft to land.

- Once the aircraft has passed over the runway threshold, the **thrust** levers are pulled back and the nose is lifted by pulling back on the controls. This makes sure that the plane lands on the stronger, main undercarriage.

- As a jumbo jet touches down, it is travelling at 160 mph.

- The brakes will reach temperatures of 200°C as they stop the plane!

- Welcome to Washington Dulles International Airport.

PILOT FACT

Pilots are only allowed to fly for eight *flying hours* in a day, 100 *flying hours* in a month and 1000 *flying hours* in a year. Flights that are longer than eight hours are called *long haul flights*.

CHALLENGE QUESTIONS

It takes 2055 metres for a plane to stop on a dry runway, and an extra 308 metres if the runway is wet.

a) What is the wet runway stopping distance?
b) Now write your answer in kilometres, and then in centimetres.

(You will find information about UNITS OF MEASUREMENT on page 29)

You are now in Washington. You have flown a total of 3672 miles and your aircraft has burnt over 78 000 litres of fuel. In an average family car this would be enough fuel to drive from the Earth to the Moon, back to the Earth and then back to the Moon again! While you are making your post-flight report, you have one final PILOT ASSESSMENT to try. Pilots must be able to read maps and charts. Can you find things at the airport using a grid map and co-ordinates?

It has been a pleasure flying with you, and we look forward to flying with you again.

PILOT ASSESSMENT

There are lots of things happening at Washington Dulles Airport.

1) Your plane is on the runway. What are the co-ordinates of its nose?

2) What things can be found at these co-ordinates: (1,2) (4,3) (2,1) (1,4)?

3) What are the co-ordinates of the passenger bus?

(You will find TIPS to help you with these questions on page 29)

CARGO FACT

The NOTAC (Notification to Captain) is a document that tells the captain about any special or dangerous cargo that may be on board.

CARGO FACT

The 747-400 is so well designed that airline cargo handlers can unload 30 000 kilograms of cargo in under 15 minutes. That's about 20 **tonnes** of freight and 625 pieces of luggage!

CHALLENGE QUESTIONS

The baggage handlers have a number of parcels to unload. The ends of the packages are different shapes.

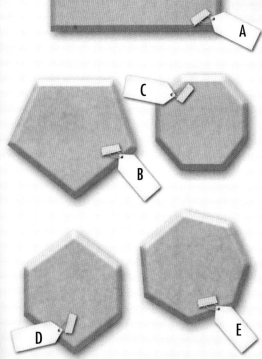

a) Name the shape which has four **right angles**?
b) Name the shape which has two pairs of sides of equal length?
c) Which **regular** shape can be made from six identical **equilateral triangles**?
d) Find the shapes with seven and eight sides. What are they called?
e) In which shape can you join all of the corners to make a star with a **pentagon** in its centre?

Cargo can be loaded and unloaded through a jumbo jet's nose.

TIPS FOR MATHS SUCCESS

PAGES 6-7

CHALLENGE QUESTION

Reading and writing large numbers:

TIP: When reading or listening to the names of large numbers, such as:

fifteen thousand eight hundred and six

it helps to write the number down using digits like this: *15 806*

PAGES 8-9

SECOND OFFICER ASSESSMENT

Interpreting a bar chart:

It is the heights of the bars in a **bar chart** that allow you to compare things.

In a bar chart you need to know what the scale is. For example, is the scale going up in 1s, 2s, 5s, 10s, 100s, 1000s or some other amount?

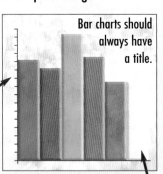

Bar charts should always have a title.

You need to know what each bar stands for, too.

The heights of the bars on the bar chart on page 8 show the numbers of passengers. If the red bar is Los Angeles International Airport, then you know that this bar shows 56 000 000. Look at the heights of the other bars in turn and match them to the numbers of passengers in the DATA BOX.

CHALLENGE QUESTION

TIP: There are 52 weeks in a year.

PAGES 10-11

PILOT ASSESSMENT

Understanding division:

Fractions and division are related. For example, finding a half of a thing or a number, is the same as dividing it by two.

If you know a multiplication then you also know some other related facts. For example: **15 x 4 = 60** and from this we know that **60 ÷ 15 = 4**

PAGES 12-13

PILOT ASSESSMENT

TIP: There are 60 minutes in one hour.

PAGES 14-15

CHALLENGE QUESTION

Imagining 3-D shapes:

TIP: If you find it difficult to imagine the shapes made by the stacks of **cube**-shaped boxes, get some small blocks and try making the shapes.

PAGES 16-17

CHALLENGE QUESTIONS

Calculations:

TIP: Before doing any calculation decide what sort of calculation it is: *addition, subtraction, division or multiplication?*
For example, if a plane travels 300 miles in one hour, and you need to find out how far it travels in one minute, you need to *divide* 300 by 60 (minutes).

PAGES 18-19

PILOT ASSESSMENT

Comparing numbers:

Here are the meanings for the symbols:
> means more than   < means less than

For example:
$16 - 3 > 99 - 95$
$\frac{1}{4} < 0.5$

PAGES 22–23

PILOT ASSESSMENT

TIP: If you are going to circle New York you need enough fuel for 2 hours 5 minutes of flight.

Using a 24 hour clock:
In the activity you will notice that the times have been given using a 24 hour clock. Look at the analogue clocks. In 24 hours (a day and a night), the hour hand travels twice around the clock face.

ANALOGUE CLOCKS	DIGITAL CLOCKS

06:00

6 am or 6:00 am

• 6 o'clock

18:00

6 pm or 6:00 pm

03:30

3:30 am

• Half past three
• Three thirty

15:30

3:30 pm

TIP: 'am' means before noon (in the morning) and 'pm' means after noon.

PAGES 24–25

PILOT ASSESSMENT

A **bar line chart** has lines rather than bars. To read a bar line chart you need to look at the tops of the lines and the scale at the side to read off where the lines reach.

PAGES 26–27

PILOT ASSESSMENT
Using co-ordinates:

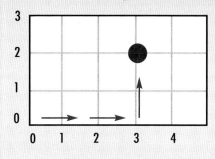

To find the co-ordinates of a point on a grid, you read along the bottom of the grid first, then up the side of the grid.

For example, a grid reference of **(3,2)** means **3 steps** along the bottom then **2 steps** up to find the exact point.

UNITS OF MEASUREMENT

We use two systems of measurement in the UK: *metric* (centimetres, metres, kilometres, grams, kilograms) and *imperial* (inches, feet, miles, ounces, pounds).

METRIC		IMPERIAL	
Length		**Length**	
1 millimetre (mm)		1 inch (in)	
1 centimetre (cm)	= 10 mm	1 foot (ft)	= 12 in
1 metre (m)	= 100 cm	1 yard (yd)	= 3 ft
1 kilometre (km)	= 1000 m	1 mile	= 1760 yd
Weight		**Weight**	
1 gram (g)		1 ounce (oz)	
1 kilogram (kg)	= 1000 g	1 pound (lb)	= 16 oz
Capacity		**Capacity**	
1 millilitre (ml)		1 fluid ounce (fl oz)	
1 centilitre (cl) = 10 ml		1 UK pint (pt)	= 20 fl oz
1 litre (l) = 1000 ml		1 UK gallon (gal)	= 8 pt

Comparing metric and imperial measurements:

1 kilometre = 0.62 of a mile

1 kilogram = 2.2 pounds

0.57 litre = 1 UK pint

ANSWERS ANSWERS ANSWERS

PAGES 6–7

CADET PILOT ASSESSMENT

The aircraft programmed into the **flight simulator** is the Boeing 737.

CHALLENGE QUESTION

b) Twenty three thousand eight hundred and sixty litres (23 860 litres).

PAGES 8–9

SECOND OFFICER ASSESSMENT

The **bar chart** shows the following numbers of passengers:
- Blue bar: 61 000 000 Haneda International
- Red bar: 56 000 000 Los Angeles International
- Green bar: 77 000 000 Hartsfield International
- Pink bar: 63 000 000 Heathrow Airport
- Purple and   48 000 000 Frankfurt Airport
  yellow bars: or Charles de Gaulle International

CHALLENGE QUESTION

You would need to divide the passenger numbers by 52 to find out how many passengers go through each airport in a week.

PAGES 10–11

PILOT ASSESSMENT

1) 6 tyres need replacing.
2) 8 ladders
3) Each cleaner cleans 47 windows.
4) 108 420 litres
5) 412 in-flight magazines are needed.

CHALLENGE QUESTION

You have walked 653 feet.

The length of the plane	231 ft
Twice the **wingspan** (2 x 211 ft)	+ 422 ft
	653 ft

PAGES 12–13

PILOT ASSESSMENT

1) 470 miles further.
2) 50 minutes difference.
3) You will travel 2579 miles.
4) You will travel 7859 miles.
5) The total journey time is 14 hours and 10 minutes.

CHALLENGE QUESTIONS

a) Atlanta   b) Moscow
c) Rome and Cairo

PAGES 14–15

PILOT ASSESSMENT

1) 54 000 kg of fuel
2) 4500 kg of fuel
3) 6750 kg of fuel

CHALLENGE QUESTION

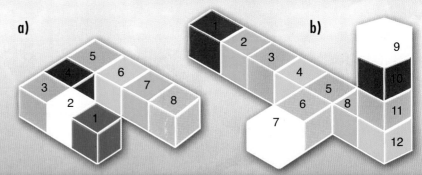

ANSWERS ANSWERS ANSWERS

PAGES 16–17

PILOT ASSESSMENT

1) The weight of the plane and fuel is 248 200 kg.
2) The maximum that the cargo, passengers and crew can weigh is 148 800 kg.
3) After 5 minutes, you will be 15 000 ft high.
4) After 10 minutes, you will be 30 000 ft high.
5) After 12 minutes, the plane's altitude is 36 000 ft.

CHALLENGE QUESTIONS

a) 7 miles in one minute.
b) 84 miles in 12 minutes.

PAGES 18–19

PILOT ASSESSMENT

1) 371 bottles   2) 1.5 litres
3) 99 cartons   4) 5 litres
5) 28 bottles   6) True
7) True   8) False

CHALLENGE QUESTIONS

a) 4 pots of tea   b) 6 litres of water

PAGES 20–21

CHALLENGE QUESTIONS

a) 2 hours
b) 11:00 pm
c) Half an hour (30 minutes) longer
d) 11:30 pm

PAGES 22–23

PILOT ASSESSMENT

Option 3: Fly to Washington Airport is the correct choice.

(Option 1 is wrong because you would need just over 18 000 kg of fuel to circle for 2 hours and 5 minutes. Option 2 is wrong because Boston Airport closes in 20 minutes and it will take you 30 minutes to fly there.)

CHALLENGE QUESTION

You would need 22 500 kg of fuel to fly (circle) for two and a half hours.

PAGES 24–25

PILOT ASSESSMENT

1) 17 500 feet   2) 4 minutes   3) 7000 feet
4) 4 minutes   5) 12 250 feet

CHALLENGE QUESTIONS

a) The wet runway stopping distance is 2363 metres.
b) 2.36 kilometres, 236 300 centimetres

PAGES 26–27

PILOT ASSESSMENT

1) (5,1)

2) (1,2) Fire engine
   (4,3) **Control tower**
   (2,1) Fuel tanker
   (1,4) Plane taking off

3) (3,2)

CHALLENGE QUESTIONS

a) The rectangle (shape A) has four **right angles**.

b) The rectangle has two pairs of sides of equal length.

c) The **regular** hexagon (shape D) can be made from six identical **equilateral triangles**.

d) Seven sides (shape E) = heptagon
Eight sides (shape C) = octagon

e) You can join all the corners of a **pentagon** (shape B) to make a star with a pentagon in its centre.

GLOSSARY

AERODYNAMICS The study of how solid things move through the air.

AIR TRAFFIC CONTROLLERS People who work in air traffic control. ATCs make sure that planes stay a safe distance apart in the sky. ATCs inform pilots about the weather and other problems and they organise the flow of planes in and out of airports.

CABIN Where the passengers sit in an aircraft.

COCKPIT The area at the front of the plane where the pilots sit.

COMMERCIAL AIRLINERS Planes that carry people or cargo for money.

CONTROL TOWER The airport building where the air traffic controllers work.

CRUISING SPEED A steady, constant speed that a plane flies at when it has reached its flying level.

FLIGHT INSTRUMENTS The mechanical and electrical devices used for flying the plane.

FLIGHT PLAN A detailed plan of a plane's journey, showing where the plane will fly, the length of the flight, how much fuel will be used, the plane's speed and the expected weather conditions.

FLIGHT SIMULATORS Machines that use computer programmes to create real life flying conditions. Pilots train and practise in flight simulators.

FUEL CAPACITY The amount of fuel a plane can carry.

FUSELAGE The central body section of a plane.

METEOROLOGY Studying weather.

NAVIGATION Working out the best route for an aircraft to take.

RADAR A method of detecting distant objects or weather using radio waves.

RANGE The distance a plane can fly without refuelling.

STATUTE MILES The official way of saying 'miles'. Pilots use this term.

THRUST A pushing force created in a jet engine, giving the plane enough speed to take off.

TURBULENCE Strong currents of rising and falling air. Turbulence can make a flight bumpy.

WINGSPAN The distance between the tips of the wings of an aircraft.

MATHS GLOSSARY

BAR CHART A chart with bars of the same width that can be used to compare numbers of things against a scale.

BAR LINE CHART This chart shows information in lines. The height of the line can be read against the scale on the chart.

CUBE A regular 3-D shape with six square faces.

EQUILATERAL TRIANGLES Triangles with all three sides equal in length.

FRACTIONS These are made when shapes or numbers are cut into equal parts. For example, if a shape is cut into four equal parts, each part is one whole divided by four, or a quarter (¼).

PENTAGON A 2-D shape with five sides.

REGULAR Used to describe 2-D shapes which have sides that are equal in length and 3-D shapes with faces all the same in shape and size.

RIGHT ANGLE A quarter of a whole turn or revolution, measured in degrees. A right angle is 90 degrees (90°).

TONNES Metric units of measurement. A tonne is 1000 kilograms.

VOLUME The amount of space something takes up or how much it holds, for example, the amount of liquid a bottle holds.

t=top, b=bottom, c=centre, l=left, r=right, OFC=outside front cover, OBC=outside back cover

Alamy: 10bl, 14-15main. BAA Aviation Photo Library: 10br, 14bl, 16c.
Dean Barnes (AirTeamImages): 18-19main. Corbis: 12-13. Tony Decker: 27. Steve Dreier: 16t.
Daniel Hamer: 9b. Joe Pries Commercial Aviation Photography: 23tc. Andy Jung: 8-9main. John Kelly: 10-11. Will Lanting: 22-23main.
Garry Lewis (ATCO Aviation photography): 1, 2, 3, 7, 16b, 17, OBC. John Powell: 24-25, OBC. The Flight Collection: 18c. Ticktock Media: 23bc.

Every effort has been made to trace the copyright holders, and we apologize in advance for any unintentional omissions.
We would be pleased to insert the appropriate acknowledgements in any subsequent edition of this publication.